M000104853

Floodgate Poetry Series
Volume 6

Etchings Press
Indianapolis, Indiana

Floodgate Poetry Series
Volume 6

Nicole and Peter Cooley
CMarie Fuhrman
Dexter L. Booth

Series edited by
Andrew McFadyen-Ketchum

This publication is made possible by funding provided by the Shaheen College of Arts and Sciences and the Department of English at the University of Indianapolis.

UNIVERSITY *of*
INDIANAPOLIS

Published by Etchings Press
University of Indianapolis
1400 E. Hanna Ave.
Indianapolis, IN 46227

etchings.uindy.edu
www.uindy.edu/cas/english

Printed by IngramSpark

Published in the United States of America

ISBN 978-0-9988976-4-6

24 23 22 21 20   1 2 3 4 5

The book interior is set with the Charter family and in Avenir Black. The cover is set in Avenir Black and Avenir Book.

Cover image by Andrew Woodward
Cover and interior design by Kevin McKelvey

Contents

Vanishing Point
Nicole Cooley and Peter Cooley

Camped Beneath the Dam
CMarie Fuhrman

Rhapsody
Dexter L. Booth

Editor's Note

I am beyond excited to release Volume 6 of the Floodgate Poetry Series, featuring chapbooks by father-daughter duo, Peter and Nicole Cooley, Dexter L. Booth, and CMarie Fuhrman. My deepest thanks to them for their work.

When selecting chapbooks for publication in the series, I ask poets whose work I enjoy if they have something they would like me to consider. Sometimes, the answers is, "I got nothing." Sometimes it's a resounding, "Yes!" Other times, it's, "No, but I have this idea…"

From there, the process is as organic as the writing of a poem. I don't worry about content. I don't think about style, subject, or length. I don't turn down a chapbook if I'm not sure how it will fit with the others. If I like the chapbook in my hands, I accept it.

Chaos, you might think, would ensue—or, at the least, a disjointed mess of a book—yet, somehow, the three chapbooks I select end up fitting together like pieces of a puzzle I didn't realize I was constructing.

How is this possible?

It's simple. The chapbook, as a form, is laser focused. It is brief but provides the poet just enough space to meditate on a particular subject or way of versifying experience. The chapbook is small yet powerful, and while the chapbook is as unique and diverse as the poets who make it, the chapbook reflects a vision of the world as it is right now—no matter how the poet is writing or what they are writing about, in the case of Volume 6: the "sudden loss of the wife/mother" (*Vanishing Point*), "the black people that in recent and preceding years have been doused and dismembered" (*Rhapsody*), and the "fusion of earth, animal, human—a one-ness, beautiful, and also damned" (*Camped Beneath the Dam*).

These chapbooks (and any of the chapbooks published over the last five years in the Floodgate Poetry Series) could easily be published on their own, and they would do so powerfully, but in the bringing together of three chapbooks by three poets (sometimes more if the chapbooks are co-written) in various stages of their careers, lives, and work, we create a unified work that celebrates the broad range of poetry being written today while offering a collective vision of our time.

I hope you enjoy Volume 6 as much as I do.

A note on our publisher and authors: The first five volumes of the Floodgate Poetry Series were published by Upper Rubber Boot Books, a small press in Nashville, Tennessee. They included chapbooks by Sarah Rebecca Warren, Derrick Weston Brown, and TR Hummer (Volume 5); Regina DiPerna, Ryan Teitman, and Paisley Rekdal (Volume 4); Anders Carlson-Wee and Kai Carlson-Wee (co-written), Geffrey Davis and F. Douglas Brown (co-written), and Enid Shomer (Volume 3); Kallie Fallandays, Aaron Jorgensen-Briggs, and Judy Jordan (Volume 2); and Jenna Bazzell, Anthony Martin Call, and Campbell McGrath (Volume 1).

My thanks to these amazing poets and to the indomitable Joanne Merriam, owner of Upper Rubber Boot Books, for housing Floodgate in its early years.

Volume 6 is the first to be published by Etchings Press of the University of Indianapolis. When Joanne informed me she needed to take a break from publishing, I wasn't sure what to do. I knew I wanted to keep Floodgate alive, but I wasn't sure how. When I told Kevin McKelvey, publisher of Etchings Press, that I was looking for a press, he leapt at the opportunity. I could not be happier with the outcome. Thank you to Kevin, Etchings Press, and the University of Indianapolis.

And thank you to you, readers, for picking up this unusual collection of verse. Not quite book, not quite anthology—I'm still not exactly sure what Floodgate is, but, as the name implies, I hope it opens you up to new ideas to new experiences to new poets and, most of all, to new and renewed dreams.

—Andrew McFadyen-Ketchum Founder & Editor of the Floodgate Poetry Series

Vanishing Point
A Call and Response

Nicole Cooley and Peter Cooley

Shark's teeth. Conch shell. Mother.
We are back on the Florida coast she loved,
at the Gulf's edge, this first summer without her.

Since I arrived in Sarasota yesterday.
I have walked this white sand beach,
following continuous, sudden visitations
of you, quick intakes of breath.

I don't believe in visitation—though my mother
will always be as far away as she is close. A white cotton
nightgown I wear now. Smell of smoke.
A miniature chair she built me for my daughters.
I don't believe in
so much of what she held close. But we shared
this horizon. This coast.

Free of visitations, I remember you,

walking the white sand beach with me.
I'm thirty-three, you're thirty,

daughters at either hand,
death a word only known to the two of us.

The water at the tide line as we wander
touches the Mexico we never got to.
But the sand beneath our soles stands,
Mesozoic. Soul of the world under my feet

bringing you back, I water walk.
I stop and start. This is how longing works.

Once, as a child, I stood at the waterline with my mother,
gripping her hand. Watched the single stitch between water and sky.

Once, in Mexico, alone, I stared across the Gulf
and believed I saw this coast, believed I saw the wooden boats

from our house in New Orleans to Merida and back.

Now in New Orleans, the sky comes down
this gold at all hours between the clouds,
lattice work where I can hang my prayers,
my poems, my memories of you—

a moment, you're standing by the crib.
Our daughter, who writes half of these words,
has just awakened, standing to that gold.
She shakes the crib bars, crying, she has no words.
And both of us rush in, to pick her up, laughing.

The in-between: there was none. No illness, no hospice, no metal hospital bed wheeled into the house, no last breath we watched, no ice chips we set in your mouth, no hand we held, no feet we rubbed, no sponge bath, no oxygen cannula, no catheter. You died alone in sudden, in quiet.

Your death—and how it wounds me to put this down
—was like the last few years of your life, a removal,
a quiet, a leave-taking of your possessions
I could find nowhere in our house:
journals you kept, the gold bracelet I gave you years back,
the fake Marie Antoinette fan
I brought you from Paris, the tiered silver necklace.

Vanish (v): "disappear quickly," c. 1300, stem of Old French esvanir" disappear; cause to disappear," pass away, die out," "to leave, abandon, give out." Related: Vanished; vanishing; vanishingly. Vanishing point in perspective drawing is recorded from 1797.

Vanishing point in perspective, sea green
muted with blue, these Renaissance paintings
in the Ringling Museum, Sarasota.
Forty-four years we held hands, together,
you and I, taking in these vanishings.

Now I am alone with a painting, "The Holy Family
with Donor," by Ferrari, late 1520's.
I bring you here to joke with me—
the donor could be Mr. John Ringling.
But Mary's hands, crossed over her breast,
bring both of us to kneel down, on this line.

Vanishing.
Lovely word for the unlovely.
Break. Unbreak.
How to keep from vanishing and what does that mean
if we say it is not
a metaphor for grief?

I would like to inscribe the ordinaries:
how I stack the silverware in the neat files,
forks on the left, knives on the right, a drawer set
to please you. And the bed made, sheets straight,
tucked down for pillows, soon after I have finished
sit-ups, the bedspread blue and taut. You chose it,
this blue your favorite. To please you.

The ordinariness of the language to describe death:

I "lost" my mother. This is what I am supposed to tell people. When I screw up at work or see people I know in the grocery store line.

Yet I love the terrible euphemism of it. I am forever losing my mother.

Because it means she is still here.

As if she is out there in a field somewhere, or behind a tree, in the backyard, just beyond my sight line on the beach.

Here, in New Orleans, I go on living
in the house we bought forty years back.
Turning in our bed to touch your hand,
I throw my leg across your leg until morning.
Except you are missing.

Without my mother, I am untethered, weightless, I am only an echo of a mother now that she is gone. I float above my life.

Hands, I keep coming back to them.
I just can't bring myself to give away

even to our daughters, your engagement ring,

your wedding ring. The engagement diamond

so tiny, but how you loved it. How it shines in my stud box

beside its companion and a pearled cross. And then there is my
wedding ring.

My friend says, "Take it off, Peter, women will go crazy for you."
I don't think I ever want to take it off.

My hands are
my mother's hands.
Veins close
to the surface of my skin
like hers. Easy access at the hospital,
she and I always joked.

With her hands,

she played piano, baked bread, killed
the bugs that scared me
when I was a child
with two swift fingers.

Her hands always in motion.

One way to stanch the crying at the beginning:
motion. I go for walks, squaring our block,
then up to the levee for a quick run.

I pace the rooms of our small house, dusting,
straightening, books haphazard on the shelf,
your tasks, your sense of order I can't restore.
And in between, my motionless depletion,
my sleep, at noon, after ten hours last night.

Now, a year and a half into grieving,
books topple each other, dust collects.
Sometimes I write our initials in it,
new lovers written on the tideline's hour.

Today began without a thought of you,
I went about my small business of prayer,
listing you with the others in the family,
then my exercises, sit-up, chin-up, yoga,
then the laundry—where my hands snared a sheet,
the bottom sheet you bought, the speckled red
we slept on years, made love on, you tucked down
morning after morning. The sheets fly to my face.

Last night as always I slept in your nightgown.
One of the nightgowns my father bought you,
given to me, my sister, for our daughters.
Your granddaughters were afraid to wear them.
I took them all back.
Mainly chaste: white linen, tiny pearl buttons
the size of baby teeth. Hard to wear and yet also a comfort.

I bought you the white nightgowns
every Valentine's Day, every birthday.

Missing you, as if you were still here,
I separate my shirts and shorts by type

in the closet, even by color as you would.
You kept our lives in order, I repeat.

Dad: yes, as always, we repeat.
We repeat our missing, in our different

ways. Nightgown. Prayer book. Toothbrush.
Cigarette lighter. Shell she saved

from our first year in Sarasota, that Alissa
and I glued into a crafts project. Shell

I save—another taken after her death this Spring
on my office desk. For me the question always is:

what objects do we keep to remember?

Or the passing object: *Law and Order* on TV,
the program you could watch repeatedly
and draw me in, that darkness of film noir,
Mariska Hargitay, bent over a body,
and then the alley, always an alley,
a living body sucked into shadow.
Someone who gets away with dealing death.
Someone who lies there, victim of the camera.

Object or victim. You would object to both. You'd claim neither.
Though yes you were, at the end, sucked into shadow.

I never shared your love of crime shows, detective fiction,
mysteries. I liked to tell you I was bad at understanding plot.

Which is true. And yet I can't watch this kind of death,
can't see or read these stories. Object or victim.

The roles for women, I'd argue with you, were only
these. And yet I'd wish I sat beside you on the couch,

in the wedge of the television's blue light when
I was a teenager and now.

In the blue light of morning in New Orleans I write this
in the blue room you had re-painted just for me
to put down these poems. It's under water blue.
When I enter, I dive into the dark,

waiting for that light I write by, I tell myself,
though only to you and to this page can I confess
it's words I get from God, answered promises.

Under water blue: is that grief? Or is that metaphor too lovely?
Dragged under: yes. Yet is blue

too much? I remember when you painted the blue room,
the enclosed porch we made a room to expand our small house.

Blue room: where my childhood dollhouse lived.
Blue room: where my college boyfriends slept.

I hate the lovely words for death: *grief, bereave, keen,*
weep. I hate the friends on Facebook posting photos

of their mothers. I hate seeing grandmothers and granddaughters
on the street, their clear pleasure together. I hate myself for hating

all of this.

Yes, Nicole, let's talk about hate right now, shall we?
I hate to see couples holding hands, that grip.
Your mother would put your hand out, I would grab it,
then there was that fastening year on year.
Sometimes I hate couples—like enemies.

Hold: from the Middle English originally: to contain, to grasp, to retain, to observe. Fulfill, to have as one's own.

And from the Germanic: to keep, tend, watch over.

The modern sense: to keep in custody.

To have as one's own. New Orleans is full of us,
the house I fill with my own solitudes.
The dresser where I set down my keys at night,
the rich mahogany you insisted we purchase
with wedding money. It has to last, you said.
It lasts, you polished it to match the teak,
adjacent, where I hoard your clothes,
the secret drawer of you I can't give up.

I imagine the contents of the secret drawer. Like the photo album I still can't look at. The worst pictures are the ones with you and my girls. I can study your wedding photo, or any photograph of you in high school, or even a late seventies picture of the four of us: you in a cocktail dress, beside a pink wicker chair. I can see that picture, but I can't flip an album page to view the unexpected.

Why have I called it here "the secret drawer"?
In other poems I have revealed the contents:
underwear from Victoria's Secret,
my purchase, but mine also the gold cross
I bought at The Vatican and wore home
to present you. A locket housing what we made,
pictures of all three of them, as children.

Grief itself
is a secret drawer
I can slide open
at any moment—
inside everything jumbled, unfolded—

Bury our words:
like the nightgowns
and the rings and
the necklaces
at the bottom of our drawers.
Like the letters she wrote
my daughters. Like the miniature
books she made for their dollhouses.
Like the hats she crocheted
for their dolls.

The empty drawers: as if she had a premonition
she was going to die. And the missings,
the white lace shawl, engagement pearls I dwell on,
staring at me from her engagement photo
on the piano, next to the photo from her obituary.
Our son took that photo of her into his room,

turned it to the wall. I haven't turned it back.

The photos are unbearable. I don't open my own albums. I don't want to see her
in a picture with my girls.

Yet on my desk at work I have a portrait.
The girls a toddler and a kindergartner. The four of us making
three generations of mothers and daughters.

I am living in the Posthumous
continuously, your presence holds me.

The piano from your childhood I've tried to play
in my poor way of bringing you back.
"Christ Is Made the Firm Foundation," our favorite,
maybe the only piece I know by heart.

And the ordinaries, potholders
our children bought you forty years ago,
afghans you knitted as if their Joseph-coats
might make us cold enough to smash the clock,
begin again, twenty-four, and twenty-one.

I see you here, in one of your Christmas dresses,
playing "Ye Holy Angels Bright," my favorite.
I sing, off key and you tell me
I sing beautifully. I say you play magnificently
while my ear picks up the mistakes.
I see you now at that piano.
That's one way I can keep you here.

Smash the clock: the Christmas dresses.
How I looked forward. How I keep the black velvet

Christmas dress with the real lace collar
you sewed in my closet now. How I wish

I could show you.

To show you this poem! Or can you see it?
Can you watch us in our interchange, father, daughter,
bringing you back, then moving away into our lives.
Is it a "fiction," is it imaginary that you watch us
any more a "fiction:" that I'm "doing well"
as my shrink insists, and just today, a friend.

It is cliché, but I have to say it,
you are here, in the stuff of the house.
I just scooped out a dish you bought
from Amazon, and asked you for the temperature
to heat up the stewed tomatoes.
"They never tell you the right temperature,"
I hear you say, and "three minutes is enough."
These are the new sacraments I'm inventing,
staying alive. Hmm, the red juice lingers
on my tongue, sweet essential for my rite.

I also hear her:

"She won't know it but would know the absence of it." About my baby daughter when I asked how she would remember my taking care of her.

Absence and presence linked.

Is this one of her lessons?

Lessons, that is the immortality of instants,
the ordinaries reduced to memories
we use and use again: scrape the lint screen
from the dryer, leave no dishes in the sink.
Leave the sign out for the mailperson:
"Please take outgoing mail." You taught me.
These repetitions are sacred presence.
When I perform them, you are here again.

I want to know if she is here. I want to see her climb the stairs in
    my house now,
to hear her voice, on the phone, asking to speak to my younger
daughter. To open a package of thread for that daughter's sewing
machine, the one she gave her. I want too much—

There is "wanting" and there is "missing."
When I miss, I put something in your place.
Trembling, I'm touched. I hear "goodnight"
carrying me to sleep. I'm praying a prayer
we said together, "The Lord's Prayer," our favorite.
You're not alive, but you are living, presence.
You come and go, but then you come, again.

Camped Beneath the Dam

CMarie Fuhrman

For the rivers and bodies dammed

Snake River Lament

Your shore is sufficient for my slumber,
and my dreams for your deliverance.
The moon awakens and rises like the salmon
that sees itself in your devotion.

In you is the argument of freedom.
Your tributed debris are souvenirs of a journey,
littoral edges and lost gypsy drift lines.
What you take you always give back.

I have ridden the white crest of your body
like red men and the surge of prayer.
Like them you are fierce and invoking,
and you are vulnerable, all at once, like a sigh.

You gather things to you like an old woman.
You are peopled with echoes and nostalgic voices.
I awake to salmon howling in your reflection
and know the damming wrought by my own.

Camped Beneath the Dam

Camped beneath Hells Canyon Dam
last night it started raining.
I moved my head outside the tent and let
rain fill the hollows of my eyes.

I never saw lightning
but heard thunder roll from beneath me,
the earth upside down, hooves of animals
bolting through clouds—
it started raining lamprey and sturgeon.

It rained so hard last night I was young again.
It rained so hard the earth moved
from the graves of my grandparents—
their bones started dancing on the rocks
dancing like hail.

It rained so hard the river was young again.
Neither of us had our second names.
We chewed dirt with our first teeth
we ran together with salmon, steelhead,
the shores lifted their skirts at our passing.

Last night the rain brought back my grandmother.
She put my head in her lap,
she told me stories. She told me carp
sucked the bones of my grandfather
her tears filled my eyes. Her braids tickled
my cheeks.

This morning the skies are clear. A fly dances
on my nose. In the flooding light I move earth
worms from the trail. Sometimes
I toss their wet red bodies back into the river.

Treatise on Red Fish Cave, Hells Canyon, Idaho Spring 2017

"A knowledge of Indian customs, costumes, histories and traditions is, of course, essential to the understanding of their drawings. It is probable that many were intended to commemorate events which to their authors were of moment, but would be of little importance as history."
—"Pictographs" by William Tomkins

Let's make the artist a woman.
Young, moccasin clad, and kneeling, ochre
staining her long fingers, brushing
rough, limestone walls in the shape
of, let's say, because we can, a fish,
maybe a salmon, though salmon weren't
why she was here, but a salmon
nonetheless, because we need one
(even just this one)
to believe ever they were here, as dammed
waters belie their ancient holdings.

Let's say she is beautiful, our artist,
and why not, for beauty depends less here
on skin and lips, as say, art
and the way her body sways this way
and that, moving with the fish in the stream
of cool air that rises from the lungs
of the cave. Let's just say

she finishes this one fish, worries
a final line, maybe a gill, working
to re-member the salmon, the last run,
last summer, the cambium peels, and the way

the young man shied, then stomped like a colt
at her passing. Let's say this makes her smile
and move further into the cave, her fingers alive,
fresh with blood-made paint, her eyes
straining to hear the sound of another heart,
deeper, that, let's say, moves her

to paint herself here, higher
in the cave's throat, where darkness hides,
narrow lines for legs, a curios head, then
she creates, the perfect circle
of a belly, which, we'll say, appears
pregnant, and why not, we are, after all
moving to the belly of the cave, the woman,
rewombing, returning, perhaps

like the salmon, to her own birthplace.
And because she is filled now
with passion (and some fear) for the dark
is truly deafening in this limestone
cavern, she has one more thing she needs
to say. She covers her hand
in that red, dark-red red that screams,
(isn't it beautiful)
and she presses it against the limestone.
Or did she whisper it soft
to the rock? It nevertheless remains,
and we think we can hear it. Even today.

Now let's say she leaves,
but let's not say anymore. For it's growing
late, and we've assumed enough, haven't we,
about words that lie still in the dark,
about histories held in hash marks
of red salmon, in the perfect circle
of a woman's belly, or stuck in the mouths
of caves? Enough of stories still in red hands,
that, like the salmon, live only
in approximation to our wonder, to dammed
water, to the sound of the wind
as it blows away any trace of her
footprints left, certainly, in the soil.

Dead Reservoir

I need to tell you something:
I heard singing from the throat of the cave.
I know you don't believe me.
You lie about things you don't believe in
like ghosts, gods, and joy. The wind
here sounds like all of those things.
Did you know wind is the last thing you'll hear before dying?
I don't know if it's a gust or just a gentle shush,
but I bet it's like the sound a crowd makes
when they all draw in their breath, *careful*,
they whisper, *careful*, for dying is a fragile
and exacting act.

The reservoir below us is dead.
It died the day the dam went in.
Twelve thousand salmon died at its base,
an offering the ancients made
to set the river free again. Twelve thousand.
Deer and centipedes died.
The sound of the river died. This cave,
eardrum of the earth, it heard it.
Joy dies loud, no shuffling out. I know you
have heard it, I know it.

An elder told me that some of us return as carp,
our comeuppance. *Better than a killer whale
born in captivity*, you say. The book you're reading
about sentient beings has enlightened you.
I'm staring at turkey buzzards in the cottonwoods
across the reservoir. I like their resolute necks,
their sterile heads; they look like a pitcher
that you could pour compassion from. A noble bird,
the buzzard, never themselves doing the killing.
Songless though, they work in silence.
Is this the nature of generosity?

There is no wind now.
The dead water only reflects what sees it.
Death reflects what looks at it as well. Listen,
I heard singing in the cave. Can't you believe
in it? You think the art in the cave is a fish.
It is nothing, it is the sound of carp, it is the sound
of the roosting buzzard, it is the sound
of twelve thousand salmon dying.

Litany

I got a rattlesnake in me
getting fat on swallowed words.
I got a rattlesnake in me,
it bites the heart that warms it
and numbs it to the teachings of my mother
who said *don't say anything
unless you got something nice...*
I got a rattlesnake in me.
Stuns my ability to speak only when
spoken to; I feel its split tongue strum.
I got a rattlesnake in me
whose cool coils circle my spleen
digesting complacency spilled in the pit
of: people-pleasing-no-sense-in-arguing
(speak in a quiet voice)
*do you know who you are talking to?
that is no way for a lady to,
I don't remember asking you,
keep the peace,
pleasant-company-minority-diplomacy
please don't upset anyone
I'm warning you
shhhhh*
honey gets more bees—
but I got a rattlesnake in me.
(Can you hear her?)
I got a rattlesnake in me
drinking vinegar, swallowing concessions, whole.
I got a rattlesnake in me, teaching me
how to sense danger
(handle me carefully).
I got a rattlesnake in me
tired of being held up,
proof of domination,
tired of losing this venom for protection.
Every day I remind myself:

I got a rattlesnake in me.
No more to be poked with sticks,
no more to meet the edge of the shovel.
I got her skin in me.
I got a rattlesnake in me.
Just like tall grass, calm rivers,
and fields of wildflowers
beneath this friendly front porch,
(watch where you step).

Eve-Grabs-the-Apple

She twirls him in her left hand, a small red, merry work of art.
It is not just superficial. She holds a bruised apple. She's read
about it in some book: a couple of these Indians up in Connecti-
cut, (before this one), was dizzied by his heat. By him, she is not.
"I do own Miss Universe. I do!" He pulls the words like the pin
of a grenade and she, she just knows things. "I *do* understand
beauty and he's not. He's bruised, opened up to wet white ribs,
riddled." (If Hillary Clinton can't satisfy her husband, she lifts the
stickers from his bruised skin.) But now the apple has moved and
he failed. He'll have to admit that when bodies first touched the
leaves of ache in the garden, he moved on her very heavily... "I
moved on her like deliciousness. I only know she is the color of
something hired." She wants to grab *him* by the pussy. The apple
pulses. According to the white oval sticker, organized crime is
rampant on reservations. No other of the four-thousand-fifteen
fruits she's held think he might have more Indian blood than the
tips of her fingers. He twists the stems of the reservations. Well.
They have high cheek bones and somewhere, someone is sit-
ting alone on a porch, Native American, but I don't know if you
would call her that by her teeth. She's lucky, with her right hand
she teaches various schools. Because she is a Native, she is more
naked now than any apple has been since. Any two. "I am OK."
That she will tell you. They don't look like her children: Maybe
this apple is McIntosh. Maybe Red. She knows, it doesn't matter.
What *he* writes...It's something bad she dreamt, something he
gave to her after being an ass. She bets he'd make a great wife.
We're all like a red bird in her hand—she is setting red in us.

*In the style of Dodie Bellamy's "Cunt Up." Sources used: Various quotes from
D. Trump and Natalie Diaz's "I Watch Her Eat the Apple."

The Problem of My Body

"They took our past with a sword and our land with a pen. Now they're trying to take our future with a scalpel." —Anonymous

I am trying to solve the problem of my body. You
are unnerved by my presence, examine me
the way airports search for weapons,
you look at me as if a thing you lost
can be found in the brown of my skin, beneath
the round of my breasts, and lower, until your eyes
become scalpels, and my body is clay you unsculpt
into your ideal—

      the first cut wrinkles my skin from belly button to pubis,
      a routine examination you'll say, but there now
      beside you, lies my uterus, then ovaries
      which you hold like a wishbone, and my hands, tied
      by your doctorine, cannot grasp the other side
      as you grunt the muddy wish of generations of white
      men and women who claimed to civilize this land. What
         knowledge lies

for you in my body that you would carve adits
like you quarry for silver, like you dredge
streams, and frack shale bones, and dam the endemic
rivers—for your power to rise, caduceus in hand an unholy
missionaries key that privileges your transplantation into this land,
this body, that you pin back together with promises, threats, and
    then hang

      as ripe fruit from the limb of a tree—acknowledge me
      as evil even as you try to claim your own rib—you are Adam
      and Adam and Adam and Adam and Adam and
      Adam and the snake is of your making—I am not
      your Eve to be banished to a barren un-Eden—
      I am trying to solve the problem of my body
      and why in God's name that deseeding is your answer
      and why when I look to God I see only another way

that you can proclaim the land of my flesh as your own.
And when I look to science I see only validations for your cuts
and when I look to the law I see acts in the name of Indian Health
Services and when I look to the tree I see it's trunk split
and scarred and when I look to the rivers I see reservoirs of
    reservation salmon
dying and dying and dying—the problem of my body

      is that it was your last frontier and when it is no longer fit
      for experimentation, for exploration, for damnation, I will not
      be able to recognize it, I will no longer know this earth.
      The problem of my body is colonization.
      The problem of my body is that it was stolen.
      The problem of my body is that it is a reservation.
      The problem of my body is that it reminds you of paradise.

Dear Body

It was never your fault. It was not how you were dressed, not your fault you developed full breasts and savage hips at a young age, or that your Uncle said, "look at that swing," as you walked in front of him, age 8. Dear Body, it is not your fault that wearing a short skirt puts you in jeopardy, that the brown of your skin puts you in the minds of others that call you exotic, consider you easy. And that because I believed them I spread my dear legs. Dear Legs, I know you wanted to run. Dear Heart, forgive me for trying to fool you. And Body forgive me as we try to forgive Disney for sexualizing Pocahontas, as we forgive whomever perverted the word squaw, invented the ridiculous buckskin mini dress that appears on a tanned body in every single John Wayne western. Dear John Wayne, I forgive you for hating horses, but I don't forgive you using fake Indians to manifest your big screen destiny, in fact, I don't forgive you for using Indians at all to make cowboys and killing iconic, heroic. But I forgive myself for the time when I was twelve and saw you swagger across the TV and thought you were the kind of man I would be safe with, a real man. Dear Real Men, I am thinking about what the term real means, particularly to my body, specifically my blood, wherein lies the DNA of generations of Native women, who now address you, who now charge you with an explanation for the scars of your scalpels and your slurs. If real equals strong and strong equals powerful, by which I mean someone decides what happens to others, then I address you. But without salutation because no salutation is unkind enough to address the decisions you made about our dear bodies. I am talking to you policy makers. I am talking to you George HW Bush. I am pointing my finger at your chest, your dear body, which is still, so far as I know, intact, or at least was when you suggested a bill to congress, which was passed by Richard Nixon, that allowed doctors to remove the uterus, ovaries, womb, ability for Native American women to reproduce. As many as 60,000. Our population fell by 75 percent. I am talking to you and to the America that allowed it. Dear America, I forgive you because, Dear America, we are still here. Still fighting for rights to our bodies for our mothers, our daughters, our sisters. Dear Sisters. Dear Uterus,

Dear Womb, Dear legs and hair, and eyes, and breast, and glorious brown skin, and luck of being born Native to a naïve America, the cuts were deep but not fatal. We are still here. Still dear. Dear Body, dear Bodies, dear dear Bodies.

Cultural Assimilation

Whereas Cherokee was Aniyunwiya
Whereas Choctaw was Chahta
Whereas Navajo was Dine'e
Whereas Kikapoo was Kiwigapawa
Whereas Extinct was Beothuk and Tukudeka
Whereas Mohican was Muheconneok
Whereas Nez Perce was Nimi'ipuu
Whereas Ute was Nuutsiu or Nunt'zi
Whereas Blackfoot was Siksika

Whereas a country already exists, fully
occupied, replete with its own
names, religions, education, tradition,
laws, boundaries, art, music, freedoms,
stories, wars, farms, trade, dead, humans,
said contacted shall be expected to subsist
behind real and imaginary borders.

Whereas dancing is prohibited and declarations
shall be written in a foreign language expected
to be understood. Whereas schools are provided,
provided that one is short-haired carrying soft-
skinned bible, whereas deliverance, promised
in a foreign hand and justice, sworn with the right
hand is only available to English-speaking people
so named by the sovereign nation who found-
ed a country of many names and nations, now
unspeakable.

Whereas we were once *the people*
we were by writ forced to become
American.

Stand

Did I mention the snow? This time
of year it can fall for days. Piling up
on the roof, the forsaken
lawn furniture, the young fawns
in the meadow, on everything
that must make a stand:
white weight on the limbs
of pine, of aspen, looking like little brown
girls in tawny dresses with leggings
beneath, feet deep as roots. This year
the temperatures fall well below
zero, and even the skin of the aspen
freezes. Brown limbs, white
limbs, strip sometimes from their spiraled
bodies, fall into the drifts, forgotten
even when the season recedes, forgotten
until another stand is made, another rising, another
copse of brown limbs feels the white
weight and fights once again to survive.

Valéria

Her mother, she told me, walked from Cantu,
Mexico. Walked all the way from seventeen
years old to Eastern Washington. Golden
Delicious, Macintosh, White Transparent, seconds
and kindness fed her. Her mother, she said
never looked back, never tossed a core. She named
her daughter by peeling a Gala, each twist
another curl, another letter, until *V* when the peel
split, and the US had its newest daughter. Valéria
was baptized by apple blossoms, teethed on onions
and learned to walk by holding her mother's
legs, the slender trunks of fruit trees. Her fingers
learned the Idaho soil where her mother taught her
that "P" was for potato and "INS" was for taking
her Uncle back to Cantu from where he has not
returned. Valéria twists the Virgin Mother
on her wrist and tells me that she prays
for Jesús, but he is not coming back, nor is her father
who made it only as far as Los Angeles. A few pesos
a day, she tells me, is what he tries to live on.
If you can imagine that, Valéria says. You can imagine
the fear in her eyes, her voice when she comes
to my office, asks if they will really build the wall—
her bag ripe with books, her essay
she hands me in perfect English, words rife
with passion and promise and I am embarrassed
by the green apple I offer Valéria in place of hope
and the knowledge I am supposed to bear, but she takes it
and walks down the narrow hallway, strong, like her name,
like light through a newly planted orchard.

Squaw

I let the word clear my throat
Squaw
I hold the *s* a little longer
than I should, let the *q* push
against my back teeth and land
flat against my tongue and back
of my closed throat. The final sound
does not move my lips

I say *Squaw*
again and I feel it
on my thighs
climbing back inside of me
finding safety in my ovaries, searching
for its home in my blood, in the gentle
lining of my scarred cervix where a decade
of knives sterilized, tried to clear up this Indian
problem.   *Squaw*

and I hear it from the lips
of white men. I hear John Wayne
run it over his big cowboy teeth
like the hungry tongue of a weasel
who's eyes alone molest
and I want to steal the word back
from his swaggering mouth
put it inside my big woman bones
hide it in my marrow, feed it back
to the mouths and the bodies
it was stolen from

to put on maps. Where it's a valley,
a peak, this earth
body *is* where it belongs, but not
lying with bold-face and colonizer claims
ill-gotten lands white-named: Nigger

Dick, Chink Creek, Jewtown, never
belonging to those bodies, misnomers,
where white-skins kill mule deer, ride
snow machines, drag trout from our lakes
and say *Squaw* like they are saying *Woman*
like they are saying Tuesday, like
they are saying nothing at all.

Feather Atlas

If you are going to collect any single thing, let it be
feathers. Find them everywhere: Along the trail
you walk, stuck in the high

web of the cat-faced spider, strumming
the harp grass alongside the dead and dying
salmon. Put them in a book,

show them to your friends when they visit. Tell them this

is the feather of a bald eagle collected from high
atop Mount Whogivesafuck and they will sigh and stroke it
and talk about one day

hiking up that mountain themselves. But they won't.

You will

call it a Feather Atlas. Call it a Featherpedia.

Call it the book-that-saved-your-life
every time you jumped, you leaped, you spread
open its eight-foot-wide vellum pages. Flicker,

Steller's Jay, robin, nuthatch, griffin, thunderbird, bare-fronted
hoodwink. It can even be

a goddamn dove if that's what you need. If you could stand
this flightless morning, you would bend for rocks. But you don't
settle for earthly matters. You, you were born

for cliffs, for ledges, for high limbs. Look for the molting
peregrine. Find the phoenix nest. Fill the pages with wind. Fill
your fist with flight.

Grandmother Song

We banked the fire and fell asleep listening to the trees drink.
Raindrops and pine needles made percussion of our tin roof.

After the storm and before the sun, we heard the earth
give way to the grandmother snag as she laid herself down.

The sound of a giant falling so near our window
was anything but startling. It was a pardoning,

it was the sound of forgiveness: a giant sigh
and a gentle crash. Two hundred years spiraled

in the rings. The cry of osprey, the song of the Nez Perce,
it was the last of its kind. The power went out.

We stared out the window until C broke the silence,
"I'll miss all the birds that sang from that tree."

Then we walked hand in hand out into the night
where we found the old sentinel, lying with purpose

resolute in her final repose. We woke this morning
to a chainsaw cavatina cutting the silent rain. Black

coated neighbors gathered 'round the old torso
like crows, muttering, picking its limbs,

carrying off the old one, to feed their own fires.

June 3, 2018

This morning I wake to the old
men in the snag outside my window.
They wear the costume of ravens,
but they are elders come back
in the smoke, in the wind.
They grumble constantly,
wanting back their filthy cigarettes,
their girly magazines. But there is wisdom
in their chatter
a certain, necessary message.

I move outside to feed the grosbeak,
to wake with the thrush, to say goodbye
to the high country for a while as I fly
toward the sea. "I will arise and go now,
go to Innisfree...," sing the ravens, though not exactly.
Perhaps it is because I am born of a mountain
Indian and a seaside Italian that I cannot stay
in one place. I am smoothed by granite and eroded
by seawater as I walk the liminal space between.
What does it mean? I ask the old men. Nothing, they say,
everything. That a home in either place leaves me
longing for the other? They laugh at my philosophizing.
Tonight I will to fall asleep on the spine of the world
and tomorrow wake up in the salt of her tears.

In the Church of Ash and Serotiny

White and red planes drop
demi-angels practicing the fall
unto earth. Into flame. Scientists
say we have an epidemic
of trees.
They call it the Smoky Effect.
That barely saint inspiring
too much good will. Thus gods will
soon appear as heat carried
in chariots of smoke
pulled by steeds of fire. In their wake
nativity of open cones and the burned
steeples of the hundred thousand
churches we've learned to worship in
all the wrong ways.

January: Silver and Glass

Look how night slips, between the trees—
from this blue-black cold, even darkness
runs. In the naked aspen, a woman.
Her arms extended, her lips moving.
I cannot hear them, but her words are daylight.

Look how the dark knots are like eyes in the aspen
whose white arms reach into the knifed air. Snow
buries the tender trunk where deer might graze.
The stars fall into the woman's hair and disappear.
White sky, white snow, white bark. Woman.

I have been standing too long at this winter window—
it is time to go inside.

Matchless

There was one night that winter
when after looking in
on gravid heifers,
I walked back through the dark, toward the glow
of an oil lamp burning in my window.
Wood smoke and wind shaped the silence.
I stood outside, my body
inches from the thin glass
where even though
light illuminates everything,
        I could not see
past that single pane
the flame
your match lit
and never will again.

To Feel Your Love

I killed my first robin when I was eleven.
I shot a silver BB through its red breast

a cherry still in its yellow beak.

As I watched her flutter and twitch
in the weeds beneath my feet,
a small red tear rose from the wound

and the heart stilled. My father,
a lover of cherry pie,

placed his strong calloused hand
on my thin shoulder and squeezed.
Pride gushed out.

I've killed for other men since,

men who loved thinner women,
darker hair, less education, more money,
other women.
They'd say: *Lose ten pounds.*
I like girls in heels. You'll like it
in the deep south. Roll over.
Can I borrow a few more dollars.
You can go back to school, later. That dog,
you didn't really like him. There'll be other
houses,
friends,
jobs—

do it for
me.

Bang.
Bang, bang.

All that senseless killing, those almost suicides,
Man, I aimed to please.

I've gone back to the orchard
so many times
since that first death
looking for the robin, so as to close
her innocent eyes—

so as to bury the pain
of killing.
The gun has been mostly abandoned,
I hunt only for myself now,
understand
there's little left of me
to offer you
but this.

Ode to the Waitress

who doesn't mind
when she is called
waitress. Who knows
serving is a euphemism
for time spent locked
in the prison next door
where the sons of the mothers,
husbands of wives serve
ten to life or twenty while
their warned children wait
for refills of Cherry Coke
and the waitress waits
until the women unlock
their clutched faces, return
smiles before giving
them a check that never
includes the coffee,
the refills, the extra
bacon on the BLT
that the cook, who looks
out from behind the ticket
window adds to the toast
before ringing the bell, free
as he is from the said same
prison where a visit
was the extra meat
the inmate rarely got. So ode
to the cook, too, then, who confesses
in bacon, who checks
his principals while he watches
the waitress talking, stealing
glances only at the tips
the guards give
such as how other jobs, other
engagements may give her more
chances to escape this prison

town and beat down
look on the faces of the just
released stopping only for directions
and sweet potato fries
before blowing by this big house
town, so owed
by its inhabitants whose
dues are paid by
the state or the fed, who
clock out and walk out
from behind concrete walls
into mortgaged walls, who,
god love them,
spend the better part
of their lives as servers
and who, like the waitress,
like the cook, like
the sons and husbands, do their time
penned up in uniforms, in support
soles, in dirty white aprons
dishing out compassion
with paper napkins one free
slice of meat at a time.

This Could Have Been a Love Poem

Who are we that build snowmen
        only to watch them melt? In the freezing
season, when winter promises
long nights of burning cold air
and constant snowfall, we build with
        the beautiful storm
that provides life for the body
we roll and stack and decorate:
        red ribbon candy smile, carrot nose, black
        buttons that watch the two of us pruning
the long limbs of the alder, tying the hand
knit scarf, our sweat buried beneath
bright down, payment for the thing we've made,
                and the tiredness
that will lie down with us in winter blankets.

And now the sun, in a different aspect,
is the death of what we dared. From our window
we watch flecks of light pin the icy skin
and red candy bleeds, like something wild,
dying, as we, its creators, helpless, watch.

Another Great One Slipped the Mooring

From my window I see a group of deer starting across the frozen lake.
I call out softly to them to *be careful,* but my words only glaze the glass
until I cannot see them at all. This morning Jim Harrison died.
The news came like the recoil of a shotgun blast,
the room grew small, like the sound of feathers landing on water.
The old dog will retrieve no more poems for us.

I never knew Jim in person, but I would have hidden in the bulrushes
with him. Let him grope my breasts and grab my ass, just to know
poetry's desperate touch, that I might teach it to my poems.
Pour the Bordeaux, another great one has slipped the mooring,
his chair still warm with his lusty heat, his pen still in his hand.

It's like the time I found the cave filled with petroglyphs,
stories in red ochre that seemed too alive to be dry, as if the artist
was just leaving, moving down the throat in front of me. "Wait,"
I called low, my voice foreign to the cavern and gone
with the mystic and meaning, gone with the maker and mine
to decipher. What is to be made of this kind of loss?

When I was very young I found my mom weeping at the kitchen table.
First it was for King, then Kennedy, at last she sobbed for Elvis.
Even my child-self understood we lived in the world they changed.
Why do we miss those who never whispered our name?
A child I couldn't know the gaps, the emptiness of the cave,
the hole in the rows of books on my shelf, a reserved space.

And I continue to lament the loss of someone I never possessed.
The deer have made it to the middle of the lake. Ten brown
figures moving against the white open landscape. Breaking
clouds introduce the bright sun; the ice grows thinner.
Let it hold, I pray, *please, let it hold,*
long enough for all of us to reach the other side.

Feckless

When I came back inside this morning, back
from taking in a deep breath of mountain
air: warm pine, musky scent of forest earth, bird
song that lights in my lungs like a gypsy
perfume, I saw my chair, my notebook turned
over on the arm, my coffee steaming still
in the morning light that returns, like myself,
day-after-day to this same place.
You'll never do anything with your life,
an old lover said to me once. I sighed
myself into place, into the hopeless light,
radiant in my nothingness.

Neither Wolf nor Dog

Do not mistake me
for a wolf. My reservation days
        were merely a vacation

into a land of understanding
where hides hung on songdog bones,
skins did the talking.

        & whites, on the other side
hope for full moons, want
        the howling me, the metaphorical

Indian, the turquoise and the medicine
learned from their TVs, stories. Yet
they fear us feral, skulking through

subdivisions, fear we
will run off with their babies, drag them
from jump ropes, jaws locked

around blonde heads. They misread poverty
        for poetry, at dusk, cry finally for cavalry,
leg traps, John Wayne films. My Grandmother

sat on her porch at dusk and howled.
Howling back, she said,
is the only way to keep them
                satisfied.

New Year's Eve

As I walk through the last blue light
of the old year, the sun slips behind
a mesa and light floods the canyon
before me. Snow lies in shadows
the sun never finds.
A gray rabbit sits motionless
beneath a naked juniper.
I climb higher to feel the warmth
one last time
but it has gone where I cannot follow.
Leaving, I watch my shadow fade into
footprints I left in the dry evening
snow. By morning the wind will erase
every trace of my yearning.

Rhapsody

Dexter L. Booth

Roots

—for Darrin Manning

No one remembers where Kintu came from.
He stepped out of the dark dust
with Buganda, his cow, behind him,
and even then his skin was desired
by the groin of another.

Call her Aphrodite.

Call her Nambi.

Call her Ms.
White
With Power.

Call her cop with jungle fever.
Contain the urge to cough
(*Cunt*)
count your blessings
like seeds.

Now shudder.

It is winter,

when all creations gnarl their roots
around the thighs of others.
A Choose Your Own Adventure Story:
      no one can reach the ending
      that isn't the beginning: you wake up
      in a village filled with so much smoke
      it is all you see for years
      your skin
      burning like an offering to gods
      you cannot hear

Apollo
yelling
Phaethon
Phaethon

where is the sun
Your mother cries

walk into the light

you are holding the rope
attached to the only breathing bovine
in the land.

What they say about being black is
not always true. This cow is not a metaphor
for women. We don't all run with our pants at our knees or
our dicks dragging behind us like chains. Sometimes
we put our hands behind our heads and spread our legs.
Sometimes an officer brings her voice to a boil
and the rights spill from her lips like children leaving school.
Sometimes genitals are ripped from the loins, then
tossed over the shoulder
into the street.

Conversation Starters or Things I'd Never Say to You in Public
 —for R. A.

False: Napoleon didn't shoot off the nose of the Great Sphinx of Giza.
The truth is humbling: the Sufi Sheik, Sayim al-Dahr blew up the nose
because, of course, *any statue of a negro's face that large*
must have been idolatrous.

These are my thoughts on Halloween night,
two-thirds into a bottle of Syrah, 20,000 miles
from home, and dressed in zombie latex that
only came in two shades of Caucasian. All this glue
and the wounds won't stick. All this fake
blood and brown Sharpie so I can tell
everyone I am a dead black guy
resurrected by the White Man Virus,
and you'll laugh.

At the end of the night Christine's friend will
take photos on the porch, after a moment
of focusing his camera say, "I can't see you,"
to which I'll respond.

That, sir, is racist.

It is a joke. It is a Sufi Sheik-Napoleon cannon-bomb
that has nothing to do with height, the number
of men you've seduced, the fact
that our lives are just expansion
and cooling; we are

the aftereffect of the Big Bang.

But I digress,
        it is dark, and I am drunk.
I am drunk and you, dressed
as a bride's maid, wearing six inch heels.
It is dark and we are friends
and I am inebriated enough for it to be

awkward that your breasts are
where I am used to seeing your eyes.
You, suddenly my height, and still
pleasant. So unlike Stripper Nick,
who will later say
he is going to college in CA to major
in brewing beer. Less than a year ago
he was one of two men fighting for your
bed in a bar parking lot.

And there's Fernando
who two years past
dressed as a banana
but tonight is a panda
or a Hispanic guy in blackface,
all excessively sexual
depending on your B.A.C.
and sense of humor.

This, of course, returns
to the dark. Scientists say that
if the universe keeps growing
outward the notion of a star
will be millennial mythology.

Imagine looking up and thinking
        the Earth is the only thing...

Remaining Fragment from *The Story of Jasper* (with commentary)
—for James Byrd Jr. and Alfred Wright

What creator should we believe in
who is strong enough to resist the whitewashing
of history? Right now we are sloshing our stolen land's flag
in the river Lethe.

The man was dark-
skinned and walking towards a gospel
he could not have known

he would be a part of. The story
ended where a god's three sons chained a man by his ankles,
dragged him three miles behind the chariot
stolen from their father.

> *I am no soothsayer, but I know*
> *these sutures we have made with*
> *our veins cannot hold*
> *this community forever.*

> *The little faith we have left is enough*
> *to hold our pants above our knees*
> *if we untie the nooses*
> *of silver and gold tangled*
> *in our fur coats.*

They dumped his body in a hole
with other dead niggers.
Called it a cemetery.

> *We have been taught to love*
> *the skin of crocodiles, though*
> *once we slit the throats of goats*
> *with prayer.*

Abattoir
—for Lennon Lacy

Because in Bladenboro a Black body hangs from a swing set,
pendulous, swaying, while sunlight entices the shadow to cincture

the remains. The flat-skulled Hill, where the cotton mill hides,
is guarded through the night by alabaster trailers

and the moon, that speechless puppeteer, leading the mort dance
with her pull—unable to migrate—to this,

Golgotha. By morning, the body is no longer

Lennon, the body is a body bruised and bored through

by ants. The blue-black belted noose

held as Lennon fox-trotted towards Death.

And now come the snowy plovers with the burden of song:
He was seventeen. He was fucking a white woman. Again

the knights of the Ku Klux Klan tighten the hood
over the amygdala of the South. The cops say

it's not against the law to put an animal down.

This tale is true: *Nihility.*

Then a crow floating in on the shoulders of creation—dot of coal, mole,
feathered gob of blood.   And this: The Whitney Plantation

now a museum.   And this:

the Holy Spirit spreading its curtain
to reveal a monkey and banana.

(Don't look away. Soon they will cue the laugh track and applause.)

Hold my hand,
let us survive by abetting

> the birds predicting this storm—
> the flutter of false-winged movement and silence,
> with its paw wherever that pistol rests.

Something is swinging—

Moon Illusion-style above the grass: this, double speak for *it was a*
hungry winter.

The Moon of the Poplar Trees.

After the last flower is trampled
—for Sandra Bland

the snapped stalks of the field peer

in their direction for miles—into the eye
of the officer, the eye of the dead

black male, of the pistol on its side
reflected in liquid marbles of blood.

Soon we will return. Soon
our shouts will ring in the bowels
                    of white churches.

But first—
        hold my hand.
Where we step the mountains shrink back;

water is stretching up through the earth and we
                are haloed with shadows

                in the rising tide—our ancestors
                swim around us.

We are something.

                *

On the back of this ocean, a dot of pepper, a crow
rowing in drunken circles, a boat
        made from the bones of brothers.

        Hold my hand

until the water is darker than any death.

(Don't look away.)

After the last flower is trampled
Let's contemplate the majesty of trees:

how they stay where they first fall,
how the seeds erect themselves in spite of gravity,
oppression, doing what we cannot; growing

back into dirt, leaves
a thousand middle fingers for the sky, the sky
that turns like a mother in the maw of a dream, grumbling

a truth: coming thunder.

                    *

Imagine holding your model pose
while beetles march along the bridge of you,
strange birds snap at your face
and drink the warm nectar

of your wounds;   a knife sings the story
of two teenagers

into your back; ropes tied to you
and people hung   like laundry
by other people.

And everything dancing.

Could you keep your hips straight
until the feet of the dead cease

echoing, keep your arms raised
after they clip the rope?

Even if they never do?

The Sanctuary

The billboards are set up all over campus,
two-sided, floating islands between metal poles.
On one side cows hang upside down,
gutted and bled out—

on the other side: Africans
strung from chains, skin raw, filthy, tight
from months of edema, weeks of starvation.
Everywhere crowds circle the billboards like flies,
pointing and snapping photos.
A woman with a megaphone yells,
        "Save the animals. We can't let this happen again."

        She travels the country for her conviction.
        I think of the Afar tribe, braving the heat
        of the Danakil Depression, with its twenty-five miles
        of salt, in search of white gold. They chisel
        their fluoride-softened teeth as a statement
        of manhood,

        I think of the Danakil
        Depression, with its twenty-five miles
        of salt—the Afar tribe braving the heat
        for white gold, chiseling their fluoride-softened teeth,

wonder if it's true that no one investigates
deaths in Congo.

                *

At the Phoenix Zoo the African lion sits, dehydrated
with his tongue out. The elephant eats with her back to the crowd.
Flamingos are tagged with numbers, stand
one-legged and oblivious to that history.

A child tries to climb the gate and I whisper,
        "See that one? Number seven?
        That one is named Zimbardo.
And the small one huddled in the corner—
they call him Somersett."

        *

Years ago, in a dream, I was approached by the woman
with the megaphone. The woman
simply set down the trash bag she was carrying and walked
off into the crowd. I opened the bag
with a stick. Inside—the decapitated body of a calf.

        *

The guide tells me, "The lion's roar can be heard
from five miles away."

        *

Now I am watching a Watusi bull
taking a piss, wondering if it could be giving birth—
        there is so much water between us. It leans forward.
The guide says,
        "Watusi cattle grow horns up to eight feet across."

I tell Musheerah about Lurch, the Watusi
with the record for largest horns, over one hundred pounds each.

She doesn't believe me, asks how they got there, how
they survive.

*How did we get here? There was a time
        when kids your age didn't think
        white people were real...*

Neo-Afronaut Anthem

"And they await,
across the Changes and the spiraling dead,
our Black revival, our Black vinegar,
our hands, and our hot blood."
        —Gwendolyn Brooks

Told we are cursed, we sing hymns and
lift our tongues to the moon. Hoping they
hear us, we dance across this barque, await
the weightlessness of unruly being. Across
the universe we fly—in an oil drum or the
casing of a bullet—we outline the changes
we have made in history with chalk and
the shape is our bodies laid across the
doorstep of their god. Our future, spiraling,
free fall planet that it is, we will find it dead
if we cannot heave this slag. Believe me, our
fables don't end like this. We know the Black
because we come from it. The trope: revival
after three days in the dark. Records bay. Our
ancestors whir; strange fruit that grew black
on the rope's stemmed branches; pour vinegar
on any wound: you'll find relief. This is not our
science. Yesterday I drew a universe on my hands
and feet with the tip of a nail. I have chartered and
mapped this body so that it is safe to dream. Our
breath will form new constellations as we sing. Hot
and dense are our voices, hot and dense our blood.

A Change is Gonna Come
—for Garrick and Carl Hopkins

Given the name of the demigods
every star dies

too soon. We confuse veins
for vision large enough to step into

like ballrooms with pearled ceilings,
chandeliers that crook down like arms,
like thumbs over gun hammers.

Something about two black
men owning property in West Virginia
means a white man can kill them
and call it an accident.

We are always trespassing
on someone's land: the body
a borrowed, unclaimable thing.
We are all born by the river.
The tent Sam sings about is an eyelid:
      secret things happen
      behind its flaps—some birth
or the naming of its opposite.

The Retreat at Twin Lakes

The son of a god wanted
to ride in a chariot. Imagine

the love—Phaethon, only a boy, mortal,
stepping onto the warm, jeweled plate
of the carriage. The horses must have smelt
of pine. Phaethon said,

If you are my father, prove it.
So Apollo gave him the reins.

Yes, the boy was a bastard, but who isn't?
The gods took what they wanted.
So do we—we take

oaths heavy like cotton, symbolic as stars, stripes
gouged into the pages of our father's backs.

Lie:

the sun came down so hard
even the gods looked away.
They won't say we screamed in pain,
but we did, our hair curling, skin
turning the way of an avocado
when it is soft and beaten.

Even the Greeks thought
we were an accident.

It ends with this:

> darkness for days,
> light coming only from the clouds,
> hoods over the heads
> of those who put the sun down.

Blackness

the punch line to a joke. On Halloween
a boy masks his face
with shoe polish, says
he's just some dead nigger. We know

his dance and song:
hoodie, red paint, friend
named George—

I'm not racist but...
A blonde announces to the world
*Black people were a lot nicer
before the civil rights movement.*

I wonder why

when LeVar Burton is pulled over by cops
he takes off his hat and glasses, rests his hands
outside the window, on the door: compliance.
He is not defeated. He knows handcuffs are just
fancy chains.

At a bar named Pranksters,
where no one is wearing your face,
the smiles are colder than the drinks
and the tree above me is dangling
colorful nooses from its arms.
When I tell the waitress
I am uncomfortable

she says
they are there to catch birds,
my black friends
sit under them
and don't complain—
your history is no one's problem but your own.

She does not say,
        "here in the desert race matters
        as much as the weather."
She does not say,

"it doesn't change, the wind
just rustles the dirt, inconveniences the regulars
who want to forget what they've done because..."

It doesn't matter anyway. When Phaethon died
his ashes were cast amongst the swirling stars.

Slurring, a white kid tells me he knows my people
go to college because he sees them
playing football. He announces his love for black
asses. At least

two days passed without Apollo lifting the sun,
days dark as coal, mountain shadow, dark
as Scientific Adam and the thoughts he brings.

Trayvon, if I marry a white woman maybe
my son can pass with your name.

Porky Pig Sits Next to a Boy in the Street

and eats lunch from a picnic
basket on a checkered blanket
the color of the nigger's blood.

The neighborhood watch volunteer made sure
        a boy is just a body now.

The scattered crows return
and bow their heads
not to pray   thanks for this meal.   No,

they won't take the body's flesh   into their beaks,
        nor lick the crusted wounds,

but the pig cleans his entire face   with his tongue
        until all evidence of bread crumbs is gone.

                That's all, folks.

        He who grows tired of clichés
should avoid 30's cartoons   and the evening news.

            [No Jail Time For Cop Who Shot Unarmed Black Man]

Operation Ghetto Storm.

            [Another Unarmed Black Teen Shot and Killed...]

Every gun is a toy

—all the dead boys are pretending.
the bullets are crazed canines.

                Freeze

while the articulated ham exits the scene

to sell his gun
to the highest bidder,

tell the media   the Guggenheim
wants to place it behind glass   preserve it
like a mother's memory of her only son.

The murder lifts the boy.
The murder buries the body
beneath the Echo Tree.

Pretend this show is not a rerun,
that we aren't shot   for syndication,
another cartoon in which the dead won't stay.

Come back.

Say it three times
loud as gunshots.

     Boy. Boy. Boy.

Angel's Glow

Listen: There is a hurt in our heels all night
that is the whistling after a bullet, the song
of a night bird cinching the spine.

Those who hear it wake to see someone
feasting at their feet as they sit up in their beds.

Listen: The night wind bawls over our bodies.
From far off the dead sing faintly, a preacher's
yell filling the congregation,

the congregation giving up
        their souls in the old spirit dance—
We say: even guilty feet have rhythm. You can see it
if you press your face to the hoods of Los Angeles

police cars. You can't see it on the dash cams but it is
being clubbed into our faces, it is
being ground into beef

paddy wagons and served to us
on platters by foxes in tuxedos. Here's to
the news of would-be-presidents endorsed

by Klansmen. Here's to whitewashing
and appropriating everything

except the   dead   and the bullet   and the sentence.

What does it mean to be not guilty? In the streets
of North Carolina bags of peppermints and Smarties
dropped in driveways for children.

Save our Land/Join the Klan—

This rain, too, loves to dance.

*

It is harder work then you'd imagine,
putting your hands up
and making them stay there. It is harder work

still, being the blood
rushing to close those wounds.

Take your pick: prick
the palms, jag between the ribs,
pry open the chest

with the confederate flagpole.
If Calvary exists, it is The Hill in Eaton
where the freed slaves yanked the nails
from the God-son's hands. Where
the only traces of our possession

are footprints in the soil beneath
praise cabins, sweat from the elder's
fingers clasped around mouths
shouting, Union soldiers
in Shiloh, blue shrapnel
wounds glowing, given
mercy from infection.

If Calvary exists, it is this:

A white officer called for a noise complaint
joining four black teens in a game of basketball.

Listen: it is not gravity that suppresses
        the dead. It is memory without rhythm.

            Look at the bodies in their black hoods. Now
watch them dance. Watch them dance.

Notes on Dexter L. Booth's poems

"Porky Pig Sits Next to a Boy in the Street..." is dedicated to Mike Brown, Trayvon Martin, and Tamir Rice.

Acknowledgements

Nicole and Peter Cooley
Gratitude to Jim Davis and Gina Ferrara as well as the audiences at The Louisiana Book Festival and the New Orleans Poetry Buffet Reading Series.

CMarie Fuhrman
Broadsided Press NoDAPL Feature: "Stand"
Cutthroat: A Journal of the Arts: "Camped Beneath the Dam"
Cutthroat: A Journal of the Arts Speaking Truth to Power Anthology: "Squaw"
High Desert Journal: "Valéria"
NASTY WOMEN POETS: An Unapologetic Anthology of Subversive Verse: "Litany"
Pilgrimage: "Treatise on Red Fish Cave, Hells Canyon, Idaho Spring 2017"
Taos Journal of International Poetry and Art: "Another Great One Slipped the Mooring"
The Raven Chronicles: "Ode to the Waitress"
Yellow Medicine Review: "Dear Body" and "The Problem of My Body"

Dexter L. Booth
Many, many thanks to the editors and readers of the following publications in which variations of these poems have appeared:
Bat City Review: "A Change is Gonna Come"
COG: "Abattoir", "Porky Pig sits next to a boy on the street..."
descant: "Conversation Starters or Things I'd Never Say to You in Public" and "After the last flower is trampled..."
Hayden's Ferry Review: "Roots" and "Remaining Fragment from *The Story of Jasper*"
Southeast Review: "Neo-Afronaut Anthem"
The Elephants: "The Retreat at Twin Lakes" "Angel's Glow"

I want to thank Joanne V. Gabbin, Lauren K. Alleyne, and everyone at Northwest University Press who worked on the anthology *Furious Flower: Seeding the Future of African American Poetry,* which included my poems "After the last flower is trampled…"and "Porky Pig sits next to a boy on the street…" Equal thanks to Peter Kahn, Ravi Shankar, Patricia Smith, and everyone at University of Arkansas Press who worked on *The Golden Shovel Anthology: New Poems Honoring Gwendolyn Brooks*, which included my poem "Neo-Afronaut Anthem."

Deep respect goes to those who have made space in their lives and hearts for the development of these poems. I'm fortunate to call you my friends, teachers, mentors, and peers. Your kindness, conversation, love, laughter, tears, edits, and support helped make this chapbook—this is for you: Diana Arterian, Rachel Andoga Loveridge, John-Michael Bloomquist, Allyson Boggess, Malaika Carpenter, Jennifer Conlon, Gregory Donovan, Norman Dubie, Christopher Emery, Todd Fredson, Christian Gerard, Eman Hassan, Mark Haunschild, Cynthia Hogue, T.R. Hummer, Mark Irwin, Darren Jackson, Richard Jackson, David St. John, Alex Lemon, Luke Johnson, Douglas Manuel, Susan McCabe, Natasha Murdock, Cate Murray, Dustin Pearson, Fernando Perez, Michele Poulos, Josh Rathkamp, Jordan Rice, Melissa Tse, Sarah Vap, and Kathleen Winter.

I would like to express my heartfelt gratitude to Andrew Mc-Fadyen-Ketchum and the team at Etchings Press and the Floodgate Poetry Series for their dedication and the hard work they put into making this chapbook. It's been an honor. Thank you for believing in this book and treating it with such enthusiasm and care.

To my family: endless love.

To those we have passed: you will be remembered.

To anyone who has read this far: I see you. You, too, are loved.

108

Author and Editor Biographies

Nicole Cooley grew up in New Orleans and is the author of six books of poems, most recently *Girl after Girl after Girl* (Louisiana State University Press 2017) and *Of Marriage* (Alice James Books 2018). She is the director of the MFA Program in Creative Writing and Literary Translation at Queens College-City University of New York and lives outside of New York City with her family.

Peter Cooley was born and educated in the Midwest and has lived over half of his life in New Orleans, where he was Professor of English and Director of Creative Writing at Tulane University and is now Professor Emeritus. The former Poet Laureate of Louisiana, he received the Marble Faun Award in Poetry and an Atlas Grant from the state of Louisiana. The father of three grown children, he published his tenth book, *World Without Finishing*, in 2018.

CMarie Fuhrman is co-editor of *Native Voices* (Tupelo 2019) and has published poetry and nonfiction in multiple journals including *High Desert Journal, Yellow Medicine Review, Cutthroat: a Journal of the Arts, Whitefish Review*, Broadsided Press, *Taos International Journal of Poetry and Art*, as well as several anthologies. CMarie is the 2019 recipient of the Grace Paley Fellowship, a 2019 graduate of the University of Idaho's MFA program, a regular columnist for the *Inlander*, an editorial team member for Broadsided Press, and Nonfiction editor for *High Desert Journal*. CMarie resides in the mountains of west-central Idaho.

Dexter L. Booth is the author of *Scratching the Ghost* (Graywolf Press, 2013), which won the 2012 Cave Canem Poetry Prize. Booth's poems have been included in the anthologies *The Best American Poetry 2015, The Burden of Light: Poems on Illness and Loss*, and *The Golden Shovel Anthology honoring Gwendolyn Brooks*. Booth was a finalist for 2016-2017 COG Poetry Award. He was awarded an artist residency at Yaddo in 2017 and another at The MacDowell Colony in 2018. Booth is currently a Contributing Editor for *Waxwing Journal*, a Ph.D. candidate and Provost Fellow at the University of Southern California, and a professor in the Ashland University MFA program.

Andrew McFadyen-Ketchum is an author, freelance editor, and ghostwriter. He is author of two poetry collections, *Visiting Hours* and *Ghost Gear*, Acquisitions Editor for Upper Rubber Boot Books, Founder and Editor of PoemoftheWeek.com and The Floodgate Poetry Series, and editor of *Apocalypse Now: Poems & Prose from the End of Days*. Learn more at AndrewMK.com.

About Etchings Press

Etchings Press is a student-run publisher at the University of Indianapolis that runs a post-publication award—the Whirling Prize—as well as an annual publication contest for one poetry chapbook, one prose chapbook, and one novella. On occasion, Etchings Press publishes new chapbooks from previous winners. The press is the new home for the Floodgate Poetry Series. For more information, please visit etchings.uindy.edu.

Previous winners and publications:

Poetry
2019: *As Lovers Always Do* by Marne Wilson
2018: *In the Herald of Improbable Misfortunes* by Robert Campbell
2017: *Uncle Harold's Maxwell House Haggadah* by Danny Caine
2016: *Some Animals* by Kelli Allen
2015: *Velocity of Slugs* by Joey Connelly
2014: *Action at a Distance* by Christopher Petruccelli

Prose
2019: *Dissenting Opinion from the Committee for the Beatitudes* by Marc J. Sheehan (fiction)
2018: *The Forsaken* by Chad V. Broughman (fiction)
2017: *Unravelings* by Sarah Cheshire (memoir)
2016: *Pathetic* by Shannon McLeod (essays)
2016: *#LOVESONG* by Chelsea Biondolillo (microessays with photos and found text)
2015: *Ologies* by Chelsea Biondolillo (essays)
2014: *Static: Stories* by Frederick Pelzer (fiction)

Novella
2019: *Savonne, Not Vonny* by Robin Lee Lovelace
2018: *Edge of the Known Bus Line* by James R. Gapinski
2017: *The Denialist's Almanac of American Plague and Pestilence* by Christopher Mohar
2016: *Followers* by Adam Fleming Petty

About the Floodgate Series

In the tradition of 18th and 19th century British and American literary annuals and gift books as well as series like the Penguin Modern Poets Series of the late 20th century, the Floodgate Poetry Series: Three Chapbooks by Three Poets in a Single Volume uniquely showcases the work of various poets via the chapbook, an often-overlooked form that captures the essence of a poet's vision and voice. Each volume publishes an original chapbook by a poet who has yet to publish a full-length collection, a poet who has published three or fewer full-length collections, and a poet who has published four or more full-length collections. In bringing together collections by three poets in various stages of their careers and work, the Floodgate Poetry Series celebrates the broad range of poetry being written today.

Other volumes in the series:

Volume 1: Jenna Bazzell, Anthony Martin Call, and Campbell McGrath

Volume 2: Kallie Fallandays, Aaron Jorgensen-Briggs, and Judy Jordan

Volume 3: Anders Carlson-Wee and Kai Carlson-Wee (co-written), Geffrey Davis and F. Douglas Brown (co-written), and Enid Shomer

Volume 4: Regina DiPerna, Ryan Teitman, and Paisley Rekdal

Volume 5: Sarah Rebecca Warren, Derrick Weston Brown, and TR Hummer

Floodgate's first five volumes were published by Upper Rubber Boot Books. The series is now published by Etchings Press of the University of Indianapolis.

CPSIA information can be obtained
at www.ICGtesting.com
Printed in the USA
FSHW021007240121
77840FS